SOMETHING HIDING BENEATH MY BED

by

BRIAN MOSES

Illustrated by
Patrick Coombes

The right of Brian Moses to be identified as the Author of the Work has been asserted by him in accordance with the Copyright, Designs and Patents Act 1988

Copyright © Brian Moses 2021
Cover and Interior Artwork Copyright © Patrick Coombes
Published by Candy Jar Books 2021

Candy Jar Books
136 Newport Road
Cardiff Road
CF24 1DJ

www.candyjarbooks.co.uk

Editor: Will Rees

Printed and bound in the UK by
4edge, 22 Eldon Way, Hockley, SS5 4AD

ISBN: 978-1-913637-84-2

All rights reserved
No part of this publication may be reproduced, stored in a retrieval system, or transmitted at any time or by any means, electronic, mechanical, photocopying, recording or otherwise without the prior permission of the copyright holder. This book is sold subject to the condition that it shall not by way of trade or otherwise be circulated.

To the children and staff of
Bodiam & Etchingham Schools,
where it has been my privilege to be
their Patron of Reading.

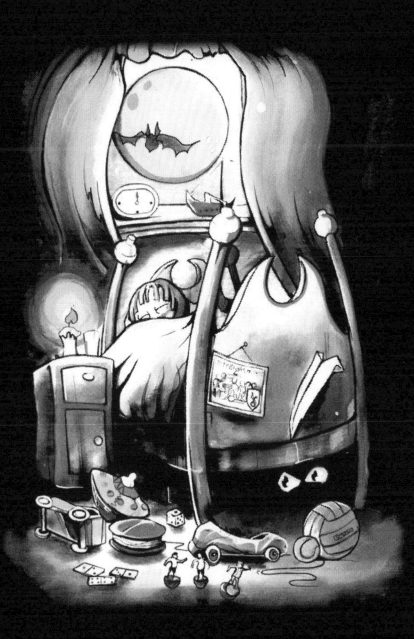

ALL LIT UP

Our dad used to go around the house
switching the lights off.

'What do you think I am?
Made of money?'
he'd say.

'I don't want to pay for lighting rooms
with nobody in them.'

Sometimes we'd wait till he popped out,
my brother and me,
then switch on every light in the house.

And when our dad came back
we'd watch him go ballistic.

Sparks flew from his fingertips,
a fire raged in his eyes.

Our dad could light up any room
all by himself.

THE BONES OF HOUSES

Something I did as a kid
was playing in the bones of
half-built houses,
swinging on their
skeleton frames,
rattling their rib cages
with sticks.

Planks of wood became
see-saws,
ropes dangled
as if someone had
recently been let loose
from a noose.

'Dangerous,' parents warned.
'Don't play there.'
But we did,
avoiding those ankle-twisting
snappy crocodiles,
and the coils of snakes
with their venomous bites
and threat
of strangulation.

It was that sniff of danger
that led us there,
the sense that somewhere
an abyss beckoned.

And I'd like to say now
that I was the one who held back,
spoke sense, took no chances,
but I wasn't, I didn't,

always sneaking back home
with the wriggle of a lie
on my lips.

Don't try this yourselves!

OUR FIRST TV

When I was young
and we had our first television,
I thought that the people on our screen
could see everything I did.

Any moment now
they'd point a finger,
interrupt the news or the weather forecast
to tell me to...
stop picking my nose,
stop fidgeting in my seat,
stop playing with my food...

I'd try to find parts of the room
where I couldn't be seen,
peeping from between the curtains,
hiding behind the leaves of pot plants,
skulking beneath the table.

I kept thinking to myself:
Had my parents installed
a spy in our living room,
to keep watch on me
when they couldn't?

I kept thinking a message
might flash up on the screen:
*Brian Moses, we can see
what you're doing.
Stop it at once,
it's a disgusting habit.*

What if they shone a torch
that peeped and probed the room
till it illuminated me?

And worse still,
what if a stray bullet
from a cowboy's badly aimed gun
left the TV
and ricocheted around the room?

And what about the Daleks
who were always threatening
to exterminate me?

I pictured my parents finding me
cold and lifeless
on the carpet.

I spent most of my time
watching from behind the settee.

It seemed the safest place
when first we had our TV.

FREDDIE CANNON

Freddie Cannon
always goes off with a BANG!
He's the sort of boy who always fails
to get the hang of things,
even simple things like
putting one foot in front of the other.
But Freddie's a blast to be with,
to rock along the road together,
watching him hopping, ducking and diving,
desperately trying to avoid
the inevitable collisions
with passersby.

He's great, Freddie, he's a mate,
but I hate it when he says
the wrong thing. In class,
in the lunch queue, or when any sort of
interruption is clearly the last thing
that's needed, Freddie jumps in,
like the *ack ack* of an angry gun,
his opinions spat out like shrapnel.
Devastating dramas talked about
for months, with Freddie banned
from breaktime, and all his favourite
games.

Maybe he'll learn in time or
maybe he's on a collision course
with life as he knows it.
And me? I'm on the outside
looking in, too timid to copy
Freddie's example, destined to fly
in his slipstream, rocked by his world
but safe in his shadow,
glad it's not me who's
Freddie Cannon,
but glad that Freddie's
my friend.

WINDY PLAYGROUND

We played blow-me-down in the yard,
letting the wind bully us,
coats above heads, arms spread wide,
daring the wind to do its worst.
We leant forward against the blow
as it rallied and flung us back,
then coats puffed out like clouds
we returned to attack the blast.
The gale drew a breath and then
pressed relentless till wild in defeat
and magnificent, we grouped again
and stretched our wings, stubborn
as early airmen.

TALL STORIES

'We've got a pylon at the end of our garden.'

'Oh that's nothing,
we've got a gasometer.'

'Oh yeah, well we've got
a weather research station
that's manned by the Russians.'

'You haven't!'

He hadn't.
So we bashed him!

Graham was always wanting to get one better.
We all knew they were tall stories,
the kind you read in some Sunday papers:
Aliens Stole My Underpants
or *Baby Nessies Discovered in Garden Pond.*

But he never tired of telling them,
no matter what,
no matter how much we yelled or thrashed him,
he'd come back for more.

Daft really, you'd think he'd have learnt.

Like after the hurricane
with everyone saying,
'A tree blew down in my garden,'
or 'We've lost the roof of our shed,'

Graham had to go and say
he'd half his house missing,
and when we took a look
there were only a couple of slates come down.

I don't know why he did it,
he knew he'd be found out,
told off, grounded.

He knew the story about the boy who cried wolf,
but nothing made any difference.

He'd tell stories about his dad too,
where he worked, what he did.

'My dad's a stuntman,' he'd tell us,
or 'My dad's shooting bears in Alaska.'

But when his dad left home,
Graham didn't say anything.

OUR DITCH

I sat and thought one day
of all the things we'd done
with our ditch: How we'd jumped across
at its tightest point, till I slipped
and came out smelling,
then laid a pole from side to side,
dared each other to slide along it.
We fetched out things that others threw in,
lobbed bricks at tins, played Pooh sticks.
We buried stuff in the mud and the gunge
then threatened two girls with a ducking.
We floated boats and bombed them,
tiptoed along when the water was ice
till something began to crack, and we scuttled back.
We borrowed Mum's sieve from the baking drawer,
scooped out tadpoles into a jar
then simply forgot to put them back.
(We buried them next to the cat.)
Then one slow day in summer heat
we followed our ditch to where ditch
became stream, to where stream fed river
and river sloped off to the sea.
Strange, we thought, our scrap of water
growing up and leaving home,
roaming the world and lapping
at distant lands.

GRANDDAD'S WOBBLY TABLES

Always in cafés
at lunch or for afternoon tea,
Granddad had a knack
for finding wobbly tables.

Then instead of simply moving
to a table that didn't wobble,
he'd see it as a challenge
to be overcome.

He'd assess the wobble,
discover which leg wás to blame
and carefully, methodically,
he'd fold some leaflet
he pulled from his pocket,
kept maybe for such an occasion,
then tuck it under the leg
that was causing the trouble.

If it didn't solve things
he'd recalculate, refold, retry.
He'd developed, down the years,
a persistence that eventually
brought results.

By the time tea was served
the wobbly table was steady.
Tea could be safely poured
and not spilt.
Grandad was satisfied.

And I've often wondered, since then,
if Pisa's Tower would have leaned at all,
had Grandad been there
to slip something underneath.

FOR MY MOTHER

She reckoned me
some kind of a disaster.

The only question seemed to be
the magnitude of me.

Was I something that sticky plaster
might solve, or was I worse,
far larger scale,
a storm, or a tsunami,
capable of wrecking her life?

The days when I was whirlpool
she kept away, fearful of being
sucked into the maelstrom.

She was wary, told me often
I was contrary, unable
to make decisions
till the problem hit me in the face.

Some days she was brave enough
to put up with me, but other days,
when my temper was tempestuous,
she wanted to hide, sideline me
out of her life.

Too often I was a tornado,
trembling the house,
when all my mother wanted was a life
that was safe and sound.

WAIT AND SEE

Dad was a 'wait and see' man.
Decisions took days to arrive.
I knew I'd get nowhere
if I needled and whined.
He'd take his time and then maybe,
when all the heavenly bodies had realigned
and the time was right
he'd say what he'd decided:
'Yes, you can' or 'No, you can't'.

With some dads, 'wait and see'
meant you'd probably be OK,
get what you wanted, given time.
Not mine. He'd need working on
by Mum, she'd get round him,
make him think it was his idea
all along.

She knew what he was like,
he'd been slow to decide all his life –
new house, new carpets, new furniture,
new stereo system – 'Let's sleep on it,'
he'd say, as if in the night
some visitation would appear
and give a sign, so in the morning
he'd know which decision was right.

Dad was always a 'wait and see' man
and sometimes it seemed an eternity -
all those times I waited to see
whether what Dad finally decided
was what I was hoping for.

THE GLOOMIEST ROOM

Sometimes I liked to sit
in the gloomiest room of our house
and there, dumbed down by darkness,
I could be as miserable as I chose.

It seemed I was attracted
to dark places,
to caves and tunnels,
to the bellies of wardrobes,
to understairs cupboards
that click-locked shut.

They were places to hide,
to crouch and wait
for any storms that were brewing outside
to pass over.

At other times, I'd challenge the darkness,
I'd face whatever demons
were holding me hostage.
I'd pretend to be a prisoner
in a dungeon, whittling away time
with memory games.

And sometimes I lay awake at night
while sleep, in a peaked cap,
checked my credentials,
held me up at the border crossing
before letting me slip across,
to find the darkness I welcomed.

ALONE AT NIGHT

Left alone at night,
the landing light on,
still knowing there are two dark rooms
that something can creep from.

Snuffles and snorts from the garden below,
screams from the TV downstairs,
imaginary eyes in the gloom,
unexplained rattles and creaks.

Something in the loft
sliding open the hatch,
tendrils dangling down and
reaching out to strangle me.

Something beneath my bed
suddenly wakeful,
hearing its breathing,
the scratching of claws.

Something in the wardrobe,
sharpening its axe,
doors slightly open,
the axe about to fall.

Something climbing onto my bed,
feeling its pressure against my feet.
If there's ever a moment to scream
it's now...

And I do...

AAAAAAAARRRRRHHHHHHHH!

DRAINS

You can play outside but don't mess about
   near drains – my mother's advice
as I unlatched the gate and looked for lessons
   the street could teach me.

   The nasty boys up the road looked
into drains, they reached down and fisted out
   pennies. I knew they'd fall prey
     to some terrible plague.

Later I learned to drop bangers down drains,
   held them fused till they almost blew
   then let them fall to the muck below,
hearing the CRUMP! of some deep explosion.

   Sometimes tankers came to the street
and workmen lowered hoses, thick as anacondas,
   to slurp and sway till the drains were dry.

   All my nightmares slunk from drains.
   Their bulbous heads and shrunken forms
     danced shadows on my walls.

   Mother said there was nothing, no need
   for worry. She talked away devils
and held back the night, but still my doubts
   came crowding back – not everything
     my mother said was right.

WHEN BILLY CAME BACK

Nobody felt safe anymore.
The bully was out to settle old scores.
Everyone vanished behind closed doors...

When Billy came back...
When Billy came back...

He was solid, built like a lumberjack.
It was permanent alert, he was out to attack.
No colours anymore, everything looked black...

When Billy came back...
When Billy came back...

And Billy wasn't happy till he'd made someone cry.
He'd twist your ear and jab at your eye,
then sneeringly say, 'You're about to die.'

When Billy came back...
When Billy came back...

Like a heat-seeking missile, he'd home in on you,
a volcanic explosion as his anger grew.
You'd be begging for mercy by the time he was
    through...

When Billy came back...
When Billy came back...

And everyone else would be urging him on
saying, 'Go on, Billy, give him one for me.'
For when Billy was beating up somebody else,
then Billy was leaving you be.

When Billy came back...
When Billy came back...
When Billy came back....

SLEDGING

Somewhere in the shed, buried under tools,
sacks, stacks of wood, there's a sledge,
knocked together years ago, in days when
snow was snow – till now, that is.
Now five inches have fallen overnight,
school's shut down, the day stretches ahead.
A real reason now to spring out of bed.
'Snow, it's snow, I didn't know,
I just don't remember what it's like.'
I really can't wait, grab some toast,
kick into my boots and zip up my coat,
pull out my sledge from the shed.
Then hike up the hill out back of my house,
lie flat down and let myself go,
skimming down fast over powdery snow.
It's one huge thrill on Breakneck Hill,
our very own Cresta run, with the snow
packed down, trodden in, mirror smooth.
I hope it will last and not disappear
as fast as it came. Our winters
will never be the same, now that we know
what snow is like. And there's time to slide
again and again, climb back to
the top, lie down and then go
over snow, over snow, over wonderful snow.

THE FAMILY BOOK

My father unlocks the family book
where the captured Victorians sit
tight-lipped, keeping their own closed counsel.
I find them caught at christenings
as the 'greats' collect with the 'latest'
and another name is tied to the family line;
or posed (but not poised) in studios,
the fathers and sons from their Sunday slumbers,
suited and sober and seemingly shy
as if their souls could be stolen away
for the price of a print on paper.

I watch my father separate the 'great greats'
from the 'great', the proud patriarchs,
the weddings and unsmiling aunts,
the fishermen released from their nets,
the light keeper and his shiny wife.
I flick back the pages and try to find
my fingerprints in their faces.

My great great granddad was lighthouse keeper at Dungeness lighthouse in Kent during the 1890s.

THE NORTH FACE

This is the famous north face of our teacher
that's never been known to crack a smile.

This is the famous north face of our teacher.
Few have scaled the heights to please her.

Some of us have tried and failed,
some of us knew we hadn't a hope,
some of us were brushed aside
or slid back down the slippery slope.

Not for her any creature comforts,
not for her any softening smile,
only the bleak and icy wastes,
of her glacial grimace.

This is the famous north face of our teacher.
All signs of weakness displease her.

But when our headteacher wanders in
and says what lovely work we've done,
there's a glimmer of something
that plays on her lips
like a hint of sun between mountains,
only to vanish again
when she starts to speak.

MR BANCROFT'S EYE

He was always giving us
the eye.

We never knew if he meant
his own eye or
the glass one he took out frequently
to roll around on his desk.

How he lost his eye, he wouldn't say,
just played with its replacement,
holding it between finger and thumb
while he cleaned it with spit and polish.

'I've got my eye on you,'
he'd often say.
'Don't think anything escapes me.'

When he left the room he'd take it out
then leave it on his desk,
propped up on an old tobacco pouch.

'Remember,' he'd say,
'I'll still have my eye on you.'

To begin with we were transfixed.

The eye held us there,
tied us to our seats.
No one wanted to risk anything,
just in case.

We thought many times of replacing it
with a marble,
with a golf ball,
with a pickled onion,

but none of us wanted to touch it.

Someone said once
they watched him removing the eye
and popping it into his mouth,
the hamster-like bulge in his cheek
shifting from side to side.

Kids couldn't wait to be in his class,
to witness such trickery, such tomfoolery.

Mr Bancroft's eye
was legendary
in our school.

FEAR OF BEING CAUGHT

Fear of being caught...

By the farmer
whose apples we took.
By the teacher
for drawing doodles in my book.

By the policeman
who always threatened to tell Dad.
By the next-door neighbour
who was so easily driven mad.

By the builders
whose half-built houses were a playground for us.
By the lady down the road
who was always making a fuss.

By the gentle librarian
for making too much noise.
By Billy's gang
who bullied younger boys.
By my dad
for scratching his precious 78s.*
By my mum
for carelessly cracking the plates.

By the ghostly ghoul
hiding beneath my bed.
By the nightmares
buried deep in my head.

I lived in fear
of being caught...

Caught without a coat
in a heavy downpour.
Caught by Grandad
telling tales about the war.

Caught by silence
when I should have admitted blame.
Caught by dreams
of possible fortune and fame.

Caught by lies
and recriminations.
Caught in a whirlpool
of hesitations.

I lived in fear
of being caught...

And most times,
usually, unfortunately,
I was...

78s were brittle records that played at a fast speed on a wind-up gramophone, until vinyl came along.

FISHING SUMMER

Michael and I were fishing companions
rushing to catch the tide before it turned,
our tackle spilling from saddlebags, our
pockets crammed with fat paper wallets of
fresh dug lug. And casting we'd encounter
familiar hazards, reels spun at our first
attempts, lines tangled, sprouted birds' nests;
we spent precious time unravelling till
tides turned and the fish bit fast. We caught an
old lag of a crab that came up fighting:
It bubbled and spat with vicious claws splayed
out like a baseball catcher, then edged off
sideways across the pier to drop-plop down
to water beneath. There were rumours too
of dreadful beasts that slithered from clefts
in search of food, of monster congers that
wrapped their tails round rocks and then gave battle.
There were times when we wished the big fish would
bite, though we doubted the strength of our tackle.
We'd picture ourselves with fantastic catches,
our photos in angling magazines, but
nothing that size ever gobbled our lines.

Michael and I were fishing companions
packing away with the light slipping by,
before cycling back through dreary streets
while darkness spread its nets all over town.

THE CARS THAT LEAVE OUR STREET

The cars that leave our street
start up in different ways.
Some cough and splutter, then jerk into life.
Some tremble and shake, jump forward
then brake. Some moan as if
they have bellyache. Some shudder and rumble,
some bellow or grumble. Some ROAR
with firepower, some shiver
and cower. Some creep along
as if something's wrong, some leap
with a spurt of speed. Some need
the magic touch, the press of a button,
flick of a switch. Some purr along
without a hitch, smooth operators,
shiny and smug. Some stubbornly refuse
to break into a chug. Some are well-mannered,
quietly spoken, but one old car,
the one that's ours, despite kicking,
pleading, coaxing, just can't be woken!

THE COWPAT-THROWING CONTEST

Malc and me and Ian Grey, we couldn't believe
when we heard someone say that in cattle towns
of the old Wild West they held cowpat-throwing
   contests!

How awful, how dreadful, what if it hit
you smack in the mouth, you'd gag, you'd be sick!
But we knew, even then, the day would come when
   we'd try it.

And it wasn't very long before the three of us
were sent away – 'Get out of the house,
get out of my sight, go somewhere else and play.'

And we walked until the houses stopped, looked
over a hedge and there in a field were pancakes of
the very stuff we'd been talking about for days.

The cows looked friendly so we started up
with a chunk or two that might have been mud
but we knew we'd move on to the slimy stuff
   before long.

Malc was the first to try it and scooped up
a really terrible lump, but while Ian was yelling
and backing away, he tripped and sat down in the
   dung.

Malc was laughing fit to burst and he must have
    forgotten
his hands were full. He dropped the lot
all down his trousers, then wiped his hands on his
    shirt.

I made the mistake of grinning too, till Malc hit my
    jacket
and Ian my shoes, and I watched it spreading
    everywhere,
while the cows just stood there and mooed!

Well, after that it was in our hair, down our
    jumpers –
everywhere! Our fingernails were full of the stuff.
Then Ian said, 'Pax, I've had enough.'

'We look awful,' Malc said, 'and we smell as sweet as
a sewage farm in the midday heat. We shouldn't
    have done it,
we've been really daft!' But Ian just started to laugh.

We laughed up the lane while a cloud of flies
trailed us back to Ian's place, where his mum's grim
    face
soon shut us up as she fixed her hose to the tap.

'It's history, Mum, it's really true. It's what they did
in the Wild West—' But we lost the rest of what Ian
    said
as a jet of water pounded his chest.

Then the water was turned on Malc and me, and
    we both went home
in Ian's clothes, while his mum phoned ours and tried
to explain just what it was we'd done.

I knew my mum would have a fit. 'That's it,'
she said, 'the final straw. No way you're going out
to play for a week, no, a month, maybe more.

'Get in that bath, use plenty of soap, how could you be
such a silly dope?* Use the nailbrush too and wash
your hair. I'll be in there later to check.'

I scrubbed and I brushed but I couldn't make the smell
disappear. I wondered how the cowboys coped
when their contest was done and everyone
  climbed in the tub.

And kids held their noses and called out, 'Pooh!'
for days and weeks and months after that, but it
  didn't matter,
we'd proved we were best, not at spellings or sport
or school reports, but at cowpat-throwing contests.

In a real cowpat contest, the cowpats were baked in an oven till they were hard and then thrown like Frisbees.

* The word 'dope' is not one that's used much now, but my parents were always calling me a dope when I did something they thought was silly.

HEAVEN

From the top of Breakneck Hill
we thought we might see Heaven,
some space between clouds where light poured through,
the place where the chosen ones would go.

We didn't know, of course, what Heaven looked like:
There were no tourist guides
and no one who went there
came back to tell.

Most of us hoped it would be an endless funfair,
a sweet store where you'd help yourself
again and again,
a Saturday treat or the sort of holiday
that would last forever.

Even the clever ones at school
had no more idea of what Heaven might be
although Sam, who lived for numbers,
said that in all probability it would be
an endless Maths lesson.

We pitied him, and thought such a geeky response
didn't warrant a reply.

So we watched the clouds playing tag
across an arc of sky,
then set off home.

Heaven could wait...
There was *Doctor Who* on TV soon,
wouldn't that be heaven enough
for one afternoon?

ABANDONED CAR

How good it was to find
an abandoned car in the woods.

It was every boy's dream
and every parent's nightmare,
somewhere dangerous to discover
how easily we could get hurt.

Fingers jammed in a door
that slammed shut,
rusted metal that easily cut
young skin.

But the steering wheel
could still be moved
and the wheels still swivelled
as if they were turning,

turning into the sort of chase
where you were out there,
keeping pace with winners
in a world-class race.

Then sneaking past
on the final bend
to claim your champion's kiss
from an anxious girlfriend.

But sadly, soon, reality hit,
this was not the Brazilian
Grand Prix,

just a car, jammed tight
between trees,
gone nowhere
for years.

CLIMBING THE CEMETERY WALL

Jake and me, we're experts at climbing
over the cemetery wall.
We do it almost every day
when we steam our way home from school.
It cuts quite a lot off the journey.
I bunk him or he bunks me,
and we hope the groundsman doesn't see
as we're climbing the cemetery wall.

There's a gap where bricks have fallen
and smashed, there's a ledge
where we stand and grip with our hands
then pull ourselves up by our nails.
But it's not an easy wall to scale
when we're loaded down with homework books,
lunchboxes and games gear slung over
our backs as we tackle the difficult climb.

I've missed my footing lots of times,
grazed both knees, torn holes in clothes,
stained my blazer and scuffed new shoes
while climbing the cemetery wall.

But sometimes, if we're late coming out,
there's a lip-curling, fist-whirling
gang of lads whose idea of fun is
fox and hounds, baying like mad
as they hunt us down
while we head for the cemetery wall.

And we haul our bags over the wall
then scramble up as best we can,
but the wall's quite high
and I kneel on my tie, half-strangle myself till I'm
 hoisted up
to lie on the top and catch my breath,
or dangle my legs on the other side,
preparing myself for the drop.

I don't suppose the residents mind,
they're pretty quiet much of the time,
though perhaps one or two, when they were alive,
tried climbing the cemetery wall!

PLAYING TO WIN

Along the length of the town's esplanade,
the arcades rolled up their shutters, prepared
for the summer trade, while necklaced with keys
like strange mayoral chains, attendants
fiddled, filled the machines and waited
for punters like me.

Pintables held no interest, nothing to win.
Instead I'd try for the cherries in rows,
a jackpot of jaffas or prize awards,
my bag in place for the tumbling hoards of
pennies that never came; or happy on
handles of cranes I'd watch the scoop
while down it dug till the snap-jaws gripped,
then whipped back quickly a cascade of sweets,
stale, uneatable, ammo to fire at
the necks of prowling attendants.

Then later I tried to beat the machines
with buttons or wire or bent foreign coins
till expert at fiddling rolla pennies
I'd leant across to receive my reward
when a hand clamped my shoulder that no amount
of turning or twisting could shift.
Then too frightened to give a false name and
address, I stammered out my lame excuse
while the manager juggled his phone and warned
if he ever caught me again he'd call
the police or my home; and abject I moved
from foot to foot till his hand on my neck

steered me over the floor, where watched by my mates
and held at length, I was booted out through the door.

A painfully true story!

ABOVE THE PIT

From my childhood room I stared at the street,
lit by the glow of a werewolf moon,
past the lorry yard to the mission hall
where tall gates were tightly shut.
Beyond, I knew, were graves in the grass,
a garden of rest that no one tended,
padlocked to keep the curious out
or sinister somethings within.

Now rough feet tramp over ground
no longer sacred. The graves are gone,
shuffled and stacked like cards
then cleared away. They levelled the land
then sank foundations, firm enough
to stand new houses.

And I wondered how deep they'd dug,
remembered what I'd read
of men who moled the London Tube
and how their spades uncovered bones,
the final homes of those who went
plague-naked to the burial place.

I was certain no good would come
from building houses in a graveyard.
Already the ground was spread with cracks,
the driest summer for twenty years,
but it seemed to me like a scene being set
where everyone's watching TV and then...

The carpet buckles, bursts apart,
an arm reaches up
from the pit...

CHOIRS

I wish there was a choir
for children like me,
children who can't sing a note,
children who growl
like they've gargled with gravel,
children with gorilla voices
who hoot and howl
and find comfort in cacophony.

I wish there was a choir
for children like me,
who desperately want to join in,
who strain to reach the highest notes
with looks on their faces
like they're in pain,
with comic strip voices
that crack the music teacher's spectacles,
that cause zigzag lines
to spread down windows,
that shatter vases,
that encourage every dog for miles around
to howl in admiration.

So why are there no choirs
for children like me,
with voices that are dire
but enthusiasm that is vast.

What joy we bring to ourselves
when we sing,
what a confidence boost
to know that we too
can make music.

SNAIL RACE

It's one, two, three, get set and GO!
But a snail race always starts off slow.
No one leaps forward on the count of two
or uses their muscles to barge a way through.

The snails don't understand what's required.
Some play dead or have really expired.
Long since past their sell by date,
they had to be prised from the garden gate,
and nothing short of resuscitation
would hurry these snails to their destination.

But others, more speedy, have some idea
of what they should do and are sliding clear,
setting off down the track at a steady pace,
while some, confused, have turned about face
and are heading off in the wrong direction
till hands reach down to prevent their defection.

And the route now resembles the M25
where most of the snails, having proved they're alive,
are steering a course of one kind or another
with one or two deviants ramming each other,
then hitching a ride on another snail's shell –
are they friends or enemies, it's hard to tell.

Then one sporty snail takes over the lead
and slimes along at a stubborn speed,
but there's no one to celebrate victory
since everyone's long gone home for their tea.

So champion snail, medal winner first-class,
leaves a ribbon of silver to shine on the grass.

CUP FINAL DAY 1961

Pete supported Burnley,
but Spurs were all that I cared about.
We knew, by the end of Cup Final day
that one of us would be leaping about
and one of us would be quiet,
unless, of course, it went to a replay.

So that Saturday in May
we sat down to watch
the match of the year.

And Spurs got off to a dream start
when Jimmy Greaves scored an early goal
and I was ecstatic
till Pete knocked me back. 'Sit down,'
he said, 'shut up, watch the match.'

It was nothing much till the second half,
then Burnley scored and Pete went mad,
but just as he sat back down again
it was Bobby Smith with a cracker of a goal
for Spurs. 'Don't shout so much,'
my mother called, 'the teams can't hear you.'

Then just ten minutes before the end
Blanchflower booted a penalty
and Spurs stayed in front 3-1.

I leapt around, jumped up and down,
ran round the room holding the cup,
listened to the sound of the Wembley crowd
as I took my victory lap.

'You're mental, you are, you're crazy,' Pete said,
but I jeered him all the way to the door.
'3-1,' I crowed, 'I told you so.'

Then, 'What shall we do tomorrow?' I called,
but he didn't turn round, just walked away,
and next day too it was like a wall
had suddenly grown between us.

He kept it up for a week or so,
wouldn't speak, kept clear of me,
and it took me that long to understand
that a game of ball didn't matter at all
it's friendship that really counts.
So I went across and knocked on Pete's door.
'I'm sorry that your team lost,' I said.
He shrugged. 'Doesn't matter anymore,
there's always next year, we'll beat you
for sure.'

'I expect so,' I said,
fingers crossed
behind my back.

THE THIRD TEAM

When I was ten, I was vice-captain
of the third eleven football team.

We spent most of our time
fighting and bickering
and bashing the goalie
if he let something in.

We spent so much time
arguing in the goalmouth
that before we knew it
they were up and at us again.

We were embarrassing,
our teacher used to say,
we always lost by double figures.
He never knew why he bothered with us.

'It's hopeless teaching you lot tactics
or taking you for football practice.
It's a game,' he said, 'you don't have to try
and maim the other team.

'Just get out on the field and kick the ball,
surely you know enough to do that.
You're just as bad at cricket,
all you want to do is bat!'

But one day we met a team
who were twice as bad as us,
twice as much swearing, twice as much fuss.
Each time the goalie let one through
they changed him over.

Soon we were winning 11-0
and every lad in their team had been in goal.

We were mighty that night, we were cock-a-hoop.
If we'd have been planes we'd have looped the loop!

We were going places, we were on our way up.
This week the third team,
next week THE CUP!

THE CROWD SCENE

They say I can't act,
they say I can't dance.
They say I can't sing
but teacher won't give me a chance.

So I'm in the crowd scene again.

I asked to be a shepherd,
I begged to be a king.
I said that I'd play any part,
any person, anything!

But I'm in the crowd scene again.

I wanted to be an angel
but all of Mum's sheets were blue.
I even asked to be Joseph
but Mary said, 'No, not you...'

So I'm in the crowd scene again.

I open and close my mouth,
teacher told me not to sing.
I move from place to place
and I watch and learn everything

so if ever someone is absent,
I'll know it all by heart.
That's when I'll step from the crowd scene
to play my rightful part.

MY BROTHER'S GIRLFRIEND

My brother's girlfriend thinks I'm weird!
I showed her my collection of dead woodlice
and the hairs from dad's beard, but she said,
'Ugh! You're disgusting.'

But what I say to her is 'I'm different.'
Any kid can collect coins or stamps
but me I'd rather collect
ear wax,
toenail clippings,
squashed spiders
and chewed bubblegum
that's been left under tables.

And anyway, I don't think there's anything more
   weird
than someone who likes snogging my big brother!

THE WRONG WORDS

We like to sing the wrong words
to Christmas carols...

'We three kings of Orient are,
One in a taxi, one in a car...'

It drives our music teacher barmy!
His face turns red as a holly berry,
his forehead creases,
his eyes bulge.
It looks as if the top of his head
is about to lift like a saucepan lid
as he boils over...

His anger spills out
in an almighty shout...

'NO!' he roars...

'If you do that once more
I'll give you the kind of Christmas gift
you won't forget in a hurry...'

So we sing...
'...most highly flavoured lady...'

'IT'S FAVOURED,' he screams,
'NOT FLAVOURED...

'What do you think she is,
an ice cream cone?'

Then to cap it all,
and drive him really wild
we sing of the shepherds
washing their socks,
till he slams down the piano lid
and takes off like a rocket
into the stratosphere,
lighting up the sky
like a Christmas star.

THE MAGIC OF CHRISTMAS DAY

If only we could have trapped it,
that magic of Christmas Day,
or stretched it like elastic
for a few more hours
into Boxing Day.
But whatever we did
it leaked away,
like water seeping through
a crack in a dam.
It was gone before we knew it,
over and out, like a friend
who couldn't stay.
It slipped off home
and there was no way
we could keep it,
or persuade it to remain.
Then another whole year
before it reappeared.

And oh how we wanted it back,
and oh how we needed it back:
That one day in gloomy winter
when anything seemed possible.

LICKING TOADS

'What I want to know is this,'
said Sharon, 'is kissing Barry Reynolds
worse than licking toads,
or do they rate about the same
on any top ten list of hates?'
So we did a survey, round
all the girls in our year.
'Would you rather the toad or Barry?'
And everyone had to answer
or Sharon threatened to twist
their arms, but Melissa said
it was cruel to go on about Barry,
and we poked fun and said,
'You going to marry him, are you?'
And then, when we counted
the votes, it seemed most girls
preferred to chance the toad
than risk kissing Barry.
Sharon said, 'You'd catch less
from the toad.' And then we said
'Let's try again, would you rather
eat a tarantula egg omelette?'
But no one was quite
so sure about that!

THE GROUP

There wasn't much to do today
so Malcolm and me and Ian Gray
planned how we might form a group
with me on keyboards, Malcolm on drums
and Ian who knew how to strum a C
or a G on his brother's guitar.

Then Ian's sister came waltzing in
with her friend Sharon and wanted to know
why they couldn't be in the group as well
and when we said no, they threatened to tell
some dreadful secret and Ian turned white,
said they could stay if they kept really quiet.

Then we argued a bit about the name:
'The Werewolves,' I said or 'The Sewer Rats'
or 'The Anti Everything Parents Say'
but Malc said no, it ought to be simple
and Ian said maybe 'The group with no name'
while his sister and Sharon said something silly
and Malcolm and I ignored them completely.

And I thought we ought to write some songs.
'Easy,' we said, 'It shouldn't take long
to think up another *"Hold onto your love,
don't let her go, oh no, no, no!"* '
And Malc kept the beat with slaps on his knee
while I played kazoo or a paper and comb
till Sharon yawned, then got up and went home.

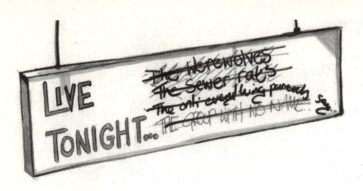

Then Ian's sister and Ian sat down
while we stood around and said what to write,
and it sounded all right till we tried it out
and discovered how awful it was.
'Let's knock it on the head,' I said,
'we'll need another year or two
before we get it right.'

And later that night on the short walk home
I said to Malc that I thought we ought
to dump the others and go it alone.
We should have seen it all along:
Two good-looking dudes like us,
we'd be famous in no time.

But Malc said we were overlooking
one small but very important thing:
Neither of us could sing!

A DIFFERENT LANGUAGE

I wish I could lose the silence in me.

I wish I could be the one who wins,
the me who fights for what I want.

I wish I could be the me who pushes words past
    my lips,
who speaks in tongues of flame
so that words I say
would burn their way
into her heart.

But I don't understand the language of girls,
it's different to the one I speak.

SOFT CENTRE

I pull her hair,
call out names,
join in all of
my mates' rough games.

I swagger past
as she looks my way,
strong and silent,
nothing to say.

I mess about,
make out I'm tough,
but underneath
I'm soft enough.

And I'd really like
to hold her tight,
pause for a while
beneath streetlights,

buy her coffee,
talk until late,
kiss her goodnight,
tell her she's great.

But I'm meeting my mates
at the club tonight.
I couldn't do it,
it wouldn't be right.

So she smiles
and I scowl,
she speaks
and I growl.

FREAK

Why do I start walking
half in the gutter, half on the kerb?
Or wave my arms like a lunatic?
Why does everything I say sound absurd?

My voice is always AWOL
Whenever I start to speak,
the words in my mouth are like boulders.
She must think I'm some sort of freak.

Why is it when I take her hand,
mine's all clammy and cold?
She's always calm and confident,
I feel about three years old.

Dad says it's just a phase
and my gawkiness will pass,
but I really do like her a lot,
more than anyone else in my class.

And thinking about it I can't believe
I've any chance of success
when I ask if I can see her again
but she looks at me and says, 'Yes!'

AWOL is a term used by the military meaning absent without leave (without permission)

ABOUT THE AUTHOR

Brian Moses has been labelled 'one of Britain's favourite children's poets' by the National Poetry Archive. He has worked as a professional poet since 1988, performing his poetry and percussion shows in schools, libraries, theatres and festivals around the UK and abroad. He was asked by CBBC to write a poem for the Queen's 80th Birthday, invited by Prince Charles to speak at the Prince's Summer conference at Cambridge University and has been a keynote speaker at literacy conferences in London and Madrid. He has written or edited over 200 books, including *Lost Magic: The Very Best of Brian Moses* (Macmillan).

His childhood autobiography, *Keeping Clear of Paradise Street: A Seaside Childhood in the 1950s*, and a children's fiction title, *Python*, are available from Candy Jar Books.

Over one million copies of Brian's poetry books and anthologies have been sold to date.

www.brianmoses.co.uk

www.poetryarchive.org/brianmoses

brian-moses.blogspot.com